I Love You, Jesus!

The Story of Mary's Gift to Jesus

We are grateful to the following team of authors for their contributions to *God Loves Me*, a Bible story program for young children. This Bible story, one of a series of fifty-two, was written by Patricia L. Nederveld, managing editor for CRC Publications. Suggestions for using this book were developed by Sherry Ten Clay, training coordinator for CRC Publications and freelance author from Albuquerque, New Mexico. Yvonne Van Ee, an early childhood educator, served as project consultant and wrote *God Loves Me*, the program guide that accompanies this series of Bible storybooks.

Nederveld has served as a consultant to Title I early childhood programs in Colorado. She has extensive experience as a writer, teacher, and consultant for federally funded preschool, kindergarten, and early childhood programs in Colorado, Texas, Michigan, Florida, Missouri, and Washington, using the *High/Scope* Education Research Foundation curriculum. In addition to writing the *Bible Footprints* church curriculum for four- and five-year-olds, Nederveld edited the revised *Threes* curriculum and the first edition of preschool through second grade materials for the *LiFE* curriculum, all published by CRC Publications.

Ten Clay taught preschool for ten years in public schools in California, Missouri, and North Carolina and served as a Title IV preschool teacher consultant in Kansas City. For over twenty-five years she has served as a church preschool leader and also as a MOPS (Mothers of Preschoolers) volunteer. Ten Clay is coauthor of the preschool-kindergarten materials of the *LiFE* curriculum published by CRC Publications.

Van Ee is a professor and early childhood program advisor in the Education Department at Calvin College, Grand Rapids, Michigan. She has served as curriculum author and consultant for Christian Schools International and wrote the original *Story Hour* organization manual and curriculum materials for fours and fives.

Photo on page 5: Bob Thomas/Tony Stone Images; photo on page 20: Phil Degginger/Tony Stone Images.

Library of Congress Cataloging-in-Publication Data

Nederveld, Patricia L., 1944-
    I love you, Jesus!: the story of Mary's gift to Jesus/Patricia L. Nederveld.
        p. cm. — (God loves me; bk. 42)
      Summary: A simple retelling of the Biblical story of Mary who poured
perfume over Jesus' feet to show how much she loved him. Includes
follow-up activities.
      ISBN 1-56212-311-4
      1. Mary, of Bethany, Saint—Juvenile literature. 2. Jesus Christ—Anointing
at Bethany—Juvenile literature. [1. Mary, of Bethany, Saint. 2. Jesus Christ—
Anointing at Bethany. 2. Bible stories—N.T.] I. Title. II. Series: Nederveld,
Patricia L., 1944- God loves me; bk. 42.
BS2490.M2N45 1998
232.9'5—dc21   98-15644
                                       CIP
                                       AC

10 9 8 7 6 5 4 3 2 1

I Love You, Jesus
The Story of Mary's Gift to Jesus

PATRICIA L. NEDERVELD

ILLUSTRATIONS BY PATRICK KELLEY

CRC Publications
Grand Rapids, Michigan

This is a story from God's book, the Bible.

It's for *say name(s) of your child(ren).*
It's for me too!

John 12:1-8

Jesus and his friends were invited to a dinner party for Jesus.

"Welcome to our house, Jesus!" said his friends Mary and Martha and their brother, Lazarus.

Everyone gathered around the table. Time to talk, time to laugh, time to eat! It was a wonderful party for Jesus.

Martha served delicious food! She was a great cook—and she loved it when Jesus came to visit.

Mary did too. She loved her friend Jesus so much that she gave him a beautiful present of perfume. When she poured it on Jesus' feet, the wonderful smell filled the room.

But Judas frowned. "Why did Mary spend so much money for this present?" he grumbled. Jesus could see that Judas was angry.

But Jesus smiled. "Leave her alone!" Jesus said to Judas. "Mary has given me this present because she loves me. That makes me happy!"

I wonder how you can show Jesus that you love him . . .

Dear Jesus, we want you to know that we love you very much. Thank you for loving us. Amen.

Suggestions for Follow-up

Opening

Greet each child by name, and let each one know how glad you are they came. Then invite children to form a circle and play a new version of "Ring Around the Rosie" with these words and actions:

> *Turn around in circles.* (hold hands; move one direction, then the other)
> *Welcome every one.* (clap, clap)
> *Quickly, quickly, all sit down.* (sit down)

As children quiet down, open one or more containers of scented hand lotion (travel-size containers work well). Invite your little ones to try a dab on their wrist—or behind their ear for fun. Let children hold the tube or bottle, and encourage them to smell the lotion as you explain that it smells good because it has *perfume* in it. You may also want to show the children a bottle of cologne or perfume with a ribbon tied around the container—let them know that giving perfume to someone is a way of saying, "I love you."

Learning Through Play

Learning through play is the best way! The following activity suggestions are meant to help you provide props and experiences that will invite the children to play their way into the Scripture story and its simple truth. Try to provide plenty of time for the children to choose their own activities and to play individually. Use group activities sparingly—little ones learn most comfortably with a minimum of structure.

1. Set out pretty place mats, paper plates and cups, and plastic spoons in your play area. Add small containers of dry cereal, chocolate chips, raisins, and small crackers. (If you prefer, use plastic toy food or pictures cut from magazines.) Invite your little ones to prepare a party for their family of dolls and stuffed animals. Wonder with them what Martha and Mary did to get ready for the party for Jesus. They must have been so excited—they loved Jesus so much!

2. Design a mural that pictures a party for Jesus. Tape a length of mural paper at eye level for your little ones, and draw a simple, long table shape on the mural. Provide magazine pictures of food and people and glue sticks. Encourage children to glue food on the table and add people around the table. Older children might like to draw themselves around the table. Talk about the wonderful party Lazarus and Mary and Martha gave for Jesus. They wanted Jesus to know how much they loved him.

3. Invite your little ones to make a gift card for someone they love. Ahead of time, copy and cut out the cards (see Pattern S, Patterns Section, *God Loves Me* program guide). When folded in half, the card will look like a gift box on the front with a message inside. Provide crayons, bits of ribbon, glue sticks, and stickers for decorating the cards. Add your little one's name inside the card. Talk about how happy someone will be to receive this gift—just as Jesus was happy with Mary's gift of perfume. If you wish, lightly spray the card with perfume to

help your little ones remember Mary's gift of love.

4. Bring small plastic containers of other good-smelling things such as rose petals, potpourrie, peppermint oil, cinnamon oil, or vanilla or almond flavorings. Let children smell and feel the materials. They might like to dip cotton balls in the liquid materials and put the cotton balls and a few petals in a small Ziplock bag to take home. Young children learn with their senses—thank God for beautiful smells and good noses!

5. Cut out 3" (7 cm) hearts from red construction paper. Make one heart for each child, adding short streamers if you wish and a dab of perfume. Sing or say "Jesus Is a Friend of Mine" (Songs Section, *God Loves Me* program guide) as children mimic your actions:

> *Jesus is a friend of mine.*
> *Love him.* (wave heart)
> *Jesus is a friend of mine.*
> *Love him.* (wave heart)
> *Love him.* (wave heart)
> *Love him.* (wave heart)
> *Jesus is a friend of mine.*
> *Love him.* (wave heart)

—Words: Adapted from lyrics by Paul Mazak (age 4), © 1974, Celebration (Admin. by The Copyright Company, Nashville, TN). All rights reserved. International copyright secured. Used by permission.

Closing

Gather your little ones around you, and assure them that Jesus loves each one. Sing "Jesus Loves Me" (Songs Section, *God Loves Me* program guide), and add the new refrain suggested in the At Home note. Invite the children to tell Jesus that they love him in a simple sentence prayer.

At Home

Find times to sing "Jesus Loves Me" together as a family this week. You may want to add these new words:

> *I love Jesus! Does he know?*
> *Have I ever told him so?*
> *Jesus likes to hear me say*
> *that I love him every day.*
>
> *Yes, I love Jesus!*
> *Yes, I love Jesus!*
> *Yes, I love Jesus!*
> *And I will tell him so.*

Old Testament Stories

Blue and Green and Purple Too! *The Story of God's Colorful World*

It's a Noisy Place! *The Story of the First Creatures*

Adam and Eve *The Story of the First Man and Woman*

Take Good Care of My World! *The Story of Adam and Eve in the Garden*

A Very Sad Day *The Story of Adam and Eve's Disobedience*

A Rainy, Rainy Day *The Story of Noah*

Count the Stars! *The Story of God's Promise to Abraham and Sarah*

A Girl Named Rebekah *The Story of God's Answer to Abraham*

Two Coats for Joseph *The Story of Young Joseph*

Plenty to Eat *The Story of Joseph and His Brothers*

Safe in a Basket *The Story of Baby Moses*

I'll Do It! *The Story of Moses and the Burning Bush*

Safe at Last! *The Story of Moses and the Red Sea*

What Is It? *The Story of Manna in the Desert*

A Tall Wall *The Story of Jericho*

A Baby for Hannah *The Story of an Answered Prayer*

Samuel! Samuel! *The Story of God's Call to Samuel*

Lions and Bears! *The Story of David the Shepherd Boy*

David and the Giant *The Story of David and Goliath*

A Little Jar of Oil *The Story of Elisha and the Widow*

One, Two, Three, Four, Five, Six, Seven! *The Story of Elisha and Naaman*

A Big Fish Story *The Story of Jonah*

Lions, Lions! *The Story of Daniel*

New Testament Stories

Jesus Is Born! *The Story of Christmas*

Good News! *The Story of the Shepherds*

An Amazing Star! *The Story of the Wise Men*

Waiting, Waiting, Waiting! *The Story of Simeon and Anna*

Who Is This Child? *The Story of Jesus in the Temple*

Follow Me! *The Story of Jesus and His Twelve Helpers*

The Greatest Gift *The Story of Jesus and the Woman at the Well*

A Father's Wish *The Story of Jesus and a Little Boy*

Just Believe! *The Story of Jesus and a Little Girl*

Get Up and Walk! *The Story of Jesus and a Man Who Couldn't Walk*

A Little Lunch *The Story of Jesus and a Hungry Crowd*

A Scary Storm *The Story of Jesus and a Stormy Sea*

Thank You, Jesus! *The Story of Jesus and One Thankful Man*

A Wonderful Sight! *The Story of Jesus and a Man Who Couldn't See*

A Better Thing to Do *The Story of Jesus and Mary and Martha*

A Lost Lamb *The Story of the Good Shepherd*

Come to Me! *The Story of Jesus and the Children*

Have a Great Day! *The Story of Jesus and Zacchaeus*

I Love You, Jesus! *The Story of Mary's Gift to Jesus*

Hosanna! *The Story of Palm Sunday*

The Best Day Ever! *The Story of Easter*

Goodbye—for Now *The Story of Jesus' Return to Heaven*

A Prayer for Peter *The Story of Peter in Prison*

Sad Day, Happy Day! *The Story of Peter and Dorcas*

A New Friend *The Story of Paul's Conversion*

Over the Wall *The Story of Paul's Escape in a Basket*

A Song in the Night *The Story of Paul and Silas in Prison*

A Ride in the Night *The Story of Paul's Escape on Horseback*

The Shipwreck *The Story of Paul's Rescue at Sea*

Holiday Stories

Selected stories from the New Testament to help you celebrate the Christian year

Jesus Is Born! *The Story of Christmas*

Good News! *The Story of the Shepherds*

An Amazing Star! *The Story of the Wise Men*

Hosanna! *The Story of Palm Sunday*

The Best Day Ever! *The Story of Easter*

Goodbye—for Now *The Story of Jesus' Return to Heaven*

These fifty-two books are the heart of *God Loves Me,* a Bible story program designed for young children. Individual books (or the entire set) and the accompanying program guide *God Loves Me* are available from CRC Publications (1-800-333-8300).